T0103597

Presented to:

On:

From:

THE
BIG
ONE

THE FIRST 52

ERIC W. A. KELLY

WESTBOW®
PRESS
A DIVISION OF THOMAS NELSON
& ZONDERVAN

WestBow Press books may be ordered through booksellers or by contacting:

WestBow Press
A Division of Thomas Nelson & Zondervan
1663 Liberty Drive
Bloomington, IN 47403
www.westbowpress.com
1 (866) 928-1240

ISBN: 978-1-4908-4911-9 (sc)
ISBN: 978-1-4908-4912-6 (e)

Library of Congress Control Number: 2014915035

Printed in the United States of America.

WestBow Press rev. date: 01/05/2015

Dedication

The Big One is dedicated to Swanora Kelly-Gordon and Carey Kelly, two of my younger siblings, who were instrumental in initiating my love for writing poetry. May God continue to guide and protect you.

Contents

Exhortation

Evangelism

Warfare

Foreword

We first met Eric when he and Judy were colleagues, teaching at a Christian school. It was clear from the beginning that he was both a gifted teacher and a man of godly principles, compassion, and wisdom. What a delight when we learned he was also a poet!

When we first had the privilege to review some of Eric's poetry, we did not realize that he had a vision far beyond personal meditations and was thinking of making them available to the public. Most poetry is personal after all, since it stems from the poet's innermost thoughts and deepest feelings of the heart. In his poems, Eric shares experiences from his life, his relationship to his family, but above all, his relationship to God. His poems clearly point out that God desires to have a personal relationship with everyone, through Jesus Christ.

Primarily, the overall theme of his poems deals with the message of salvation and the importance of recognizing the need for a Savior—before it's too late. Through the use of poetry, Eric is able to describe that message very succinctly and with great fervor. Sometimes the poems read like the Psalms and at other times, as modern-day proverbs. In addition, through some of his poems, he teases us with glimpses of Jamaica, his beloved motherland. This collection will be a great source of inspiration and encouragement to the believer and soul-searching, prompting for the unbeliever.

Manfred and Judy Kory
August, 2014

Preface

It was when I was going to high school and living in Portland, Jamaica, that I found myself writing poetry. These poems were mainly about how the Lord was watching over Swanora and Carey, my younger siblings. The poems flowed from my concern for their welfare as I was not living with my family at the time. I had assumed a fatherly role for them because my parents were separated. I even assumed the role of spiritual guardian; interestingly, I had not even accepted Jesus Christ as Lord and Savior as yet. Shortly afterward, I became a Christian through the instrumentality of my high school religious education teacher. She explained to the class how we could pray and ask Jesus to forgive us of our sins and receive Him as Lord and Savior. I said the prayer and believed that I was saved.

After I accepted Christ, my love for sharing the gospel began to grow. Naturally, evangelism and poetry were married. In a short time, I got involved in street evangelism through two local church groups. Eventually, I was used to lead both siblings to the Lord. Several years later, I had the opportunity to lead my daughters to the Lord. I was delighted when one of my nieces phoned to ask if I would lead her in saying the sinner's prayer. The Lord had also given me the privilege to work with Him to lead several strangers, through group or personal evangelism, to a saving knowledge of Christ. Over the past five years, I have been a member of an evangelism group, from my present church, which shares Christ in Washington D.C., on a regular basis.

After a few decades of writing, I began to read my poems at churches and various Christian gatherings. Recently, I felt that I should make the poems available to a wider audience. What began as a private family affair has developed into a public assignment in which the benefit of the church and the glory of the Lord are paramount. *The Big One* may be given as a gift, used as the basis for group discussion, or read for personal comfort, challenge, and inspiration.

Acknowledgement

Special thanks to Jesus Christ for going to the cross for me.

Many people have influenced the writing of this volume of poems directly and indirectly; I want to express my appreciation to all concerned.

My wife Viviene, and my daughters, Romae and Latoi, have been a consistent and stable source of support. Through my parents, Patrick and Hilda Kelly and my siblings Dennis, Lorna, Marcia, Swanora, and Carey, my foundational values were forged. Thanks also to my brother-in law, Kenton Gordon, who has been a true friend to me.

There are many other persons who have helped me in my Christian walk. Thanks to: Miss Veronica Walker, from Portland, Jamaica, who was like a second mother to me. Two of her children, Winston Doyley and Medorah Doyley, have played significant roles in my spiritual development. Mrs. Delrose Ogilvie, Dr. Walter Hayes, and Pastor Julian Dangerfield have all had positive impact on my Christian growth. I also want to thank the members of my home church, Heritage Fellowship Church in Reston, VA, for their support over the past seven years; special thanks goes to Senior Pastor, Reverend Dr. Norman A. Tate, for the spiritual nourishment he gives to my family on a weekly basis.

There are those who have helped with the preparation of the manuscript. Thanks to my daughter Romae and my niece Kaelor Gordon for typing the first draft. Miss Sarah Madden has also helped in the initial editing of the poems. I am grateful to Mrs. Sheila Woodward for meticulously and efficiently editing the first e-proof. I am grateful to Mr. and Mrs. Manfred Kory from Leesburg, VA, for writing the foreword for *The Big One*. Even If I have failed to mention your name, be assured that I have not forgotten you, and that I am indebted to you.

Introduction

The Big One is a unique exploration of a wide array of profound truths that are essential for the journey of a disciple of Christ. I emphasized the significance of the qualities of gratitude and joy. From a biblical perspective, I investigated the value of prayer as a vehicle that transports one from a destiny of eternal agony to one of everlasting bliss. I considered the importance of faith as a key ingredient for the appropriation of the victory secured by Christ.

The Big One asks some thought–provoking questions that we often push to the far recesses of our minds. Some of these questions are presented here. What kinds of thoughts consistently consume our minds? What are the inherent risks involved in choosing a mate? How can we discover and fulfill our assignments? Furthermore, I explored one of the chief functions of the Christian Church- evangelism. In addition, I scrutinized the potency of the weapons of spiritual warfare.

Lastly, I celebrated the sacrifice made for the redemption of mankind, set in the context of struggles, and the ultimate victory for Christ and his followers. Directly and indirectly, the focus of these poems is on the One Who will eternally carry scars as a result of the price He paid for the gift of righteousness and the abundance of grace for His brethren.

Thanksgiving

Give Thanks

*T*hank you Lord, for all
That you have done;
Thank you Lord, for
Sending your Son.

Thank you Lord, for
Making me whole;
Thank you Lord, for
Saving my soul.

Thank you Lord, for
Being my Rock;
Thank you Lord, for
Setting my clock.

Thank you for peace in
Life and eternity;
Thank you Lord, for
My journey and destiny.

When I think of the
Goodness of God,
I have no need to be
Worried, unhappy, or sad.

Let me not take
The shed blood for granted,
But be thankful, joyful,
And gracious instead.

Shout for the Lord

*L*ift your hands and
Praise the Lord;
Tell of His might and
The truth of His word.

Cry with a loud
Voice and shout,
Tell the nations what
His love is about.

Do not wait until
You are in heaven
To tell of the joy
His salvation has given.

Tell the congregation of His
Miracles through the ages,
As you work, you are
Increasing your wages.

Remind the people that
Salvation comes by faith,
Not because you're loyal,
Mighty, or great.

Lift your voices, blow
Your trumpet and cry,
For in vain the Holy
Son will not die.

Rejoice

R ejoice. Again, I say rejoice,
   Rejoice if things seem to fall apart;
Again, I say rejoice always
Because Jesus is in your heart.

Read the word,
Pray without ceasing,
But always rejoice,
To God this is pleasing.

Rejoice if your spouse does
Not come home at night;
Rejoice if you have no job,
Or your child rejects the Light.

Rejoice because your name
Is written in heaven;
Rejoice for the salvation
Your Savior has given.

What can you change
Through worry and fear?
Rejoice because Jesus your
Refuge and strength is near.

Rejoice if you do not
Know what tomorrow brings;
Your God holds the future,
Therefore, sail on His Wings.

Comfort and Prayer

Who Is My Christ?

Who is your Christ?
And what's His aim?
Where is He from, and
What is His name?

Will He protect you when
Your back is against the wall?
Where does he live, and
What's His plan when you fall?

My Christ is the Rock of ages,
The only Anchor of my soul,
He brought redemption for
Mankind as a whole.

He is Jesus, the root of David,
The Bread unleavened
Sent by the Father from
His throne in heaven.

The Christ in me is a Comforter,
Replacing captivity with zeal,
By binding and crushing
The enemy with His heel.

God is Not Dead

God is not dead,
He is alive,
God is not dead,
He is alive.

He hears and answers
Many a prayer,
He is our precious
Lord and Savior.

He sees our joy,
And shares our sorrows,
He said, "Your value is
More than many sparrows."

He knows our pains
And can heal any sickness;
God is our helper,
He is our righteousness.

He speaks His words
And proclaims our rights;
Where there is darkness
He sends glory and light.

The Word of God

H ow sweet is God's Word
     In the believer's ear,
It instills love and joy
But repels anger and fear.

It's nicer than coconut water
And curried goat;
It's better than apple pie
Or a vacation on a boat.

I like to listen to
Dr. J, Vernon McGee,
Oh God, raise up more
Teachers like him, I pray thee.

I like to listen to
R.W. Schambach,
Who said, "You have no
Trouble if Jesus is your Rock."

Through the Word we have
Peace, joy, and wealth;
Through the Word we receive
Instruction, wisdom, and health.

Weapons of Mass Protection (WMP)

We have the Ace, the King,
The Queen, and the Jack;
We can counter any type of
Shrewd, spiritual attack.

If the dark prince sends demons,
We put them to shame
By calling upon Jesus-
The most glorious name.

When the enemy sends
Discouragement and loneliness,
He will face our Jack-
The testimonies of God's goodness.

When the enemy sends
All types of accusations like a flood,
We release our Queen,
Which is His pure and potent blood?

When the enemy sends
Danger, doubt, and disaster,
We utilize our King - the Word;
This causes fear to scatter.

When the enemy comes
To steal, kill, and destroy,
He'll meet our Ace, the Holy Spirit,
Who has resurrection power to deploy.

Family Prayer 1

OH God,
We pray for wisdom, knowledge,
And understanding,
For your counsel and might,
And for the fear of the Lord.
We pray for hope,
Faith, and love.
Oh Father, give us prosperity
And favor with man
And with you.
Make us instruments of your
Love, joy, peace,
Goodness, and gentleness.
In Jesus' name,
Amen.

Family Prayer 2

Oh Lord, we do not
Know what is happening,
It's as if everywhere we go
Several fires are burning.

Lord, please show us
The right and perfect way,
We want to see
The light of the day.

We feel pain in
Every vessel of our hearts,
We don't want our family
To be torn apart.

Lord, please create
An open door;
We want to get
Off the broken floor.

The battle is too great,
It's yours not ours;
Make a way for us
To experience your showers.

Oh Father, we certainly
Need a breakthrough
Which no one but
You are able to do.

The Sinner's Prayer

Oh God, I believe
You sent your Son
Into the world to
Die for my sins;
I believe He rose to
Give me eternal life.
I cannot save myself.
I repent of my sins
And receive Him
Into my heart.
I ask Him to be my
Savior and Lord.
In Jesus' name,
Amen.

Faith

Victory

*T*hey say you have failed,
 They say you're hopeless - you will die.
They say your dreams are buried,
Tell them it's a lame, lousy lie.

The verdict is out - you're guilty,
They can see the electric chair,
Your cancer is like a flooded river,
Friends, doctors, they all disappear.

All appeals are exhausted,
You killed time, rebelled, and fell;
Be ready for your incarnation,
Take your place in hell.

Listen! That's a thunderous sound,
Shaking, breaking the establishment;
A mistrial appears, you're clothed
In mercy instead of judgment.

Goliath trembles and falls as
Truth destroys a lame, lousy lie.
The fight is fixed,
The Davids do not die.

The Key

I lost a bunch of keys at a store,
But I did not panic,
For I know that to worry
Is one of the devil's tricks.

The keys were for my home,
My church, and my car;
Without their use,
I know I cannot get far.

I was sure that I
Would find them again;
Certain, although not seeing them,
I made a claim in Jesus' name.

I went straight to the
Customer service counter,
Asked and answered a few questions,
Knowing I was the owner.

The key is not my will but God's will,
The key is hearing from God,
The key is obedience,
The key is exercising faith,
The key is taking action,
The key is trusting,
The key is resting in God,
The key is being filled with the Holy Spirit,
The key is living one day at a time,

The key is love,
The key is light,
The key is being the salt of the world,
The key is keep breathing,
 The key is brokenness,
The key is vulnerability,
The key is in your hand,
The key is opening the door,
The key is Christ.

Reflection

The Cure

M ankind has conquered
Cloning, the moon, and Mars;
Can they overcome death,
Terrorism, and wars?

One embraces death
In a suicide mission;
Another is scared
Of his final destination.

Fear of death gives
The enemy ammunition;
We must disarm
Their destructive ambition.

Some will dare to die
For freedom and for peace,
From various wars,
Oh God, give us release.

I heard that the Great Physician
invented a cure for war, and death;
If this is really true,
He is our only hope yet.

Lost Thought I

Who hung the sun and
The moon in the sky?
Do we think of the One
Who sent His Son to die?

We are obsessed with beauty,
So we insure our faces;
What about the majesty
And wonder of God's graces?

We dream of broad shoulders,
And augmented breasts;
What about the purity of
The hearts within our chests?

We tighten and enlarge
Various parts of our bodies;
How much thought do we give
To eternal truths and mysteries?

We talk about brand names-
Expensive clothes and shoes;
What about the faithful feet
That spread the Good News?

Do our hearts, minds, and souls
Seek after the Creator?
Have His words and purpose
Affected our thoughts and behavior?

Lost Thought II

*J*ust like a child who discards
   A gift and clings to the packing,
We sometimes ignore the treasure
And become obsessed with the wrapping.

We emphasize the physical
As if that is the whole;
Remind us Lord, that we
Also have a spirit and a soul.

We'll die for things that
Last for a short time,
While jewels of eternity
Are absent from our minds.

We fear those who
Can kill only the body;
But to lose the soul and
Gain the world is misery.

The things that are seen
Are temporal and finite,
But we must trust in
The one Who is infinite.

The Reason

What can you give
To show appreciation
For the everlasting gift
Of the Master's salvation?

Can anything be compared
To Christ's redemption?
How can you give thanks
For God's reconciliation?

God gave his Son to the world,
And, with Him, freely gives all things;
That's the reason we dance,
Serve, shout, and sing.

Love, gratitude, and thanks
You can show,
When to the highways
And byways you go.

You can share the great
Gift of salvation with
Your family and friends,
Then with each nation.

My Mother

I need my mother,
I need my mother.
An aching heart
Yearns for her shelter.

Having gone around
The mysterious corner,
I believe I'll see her
When I cross the river.

I can still see the love
In her inquiring eyes
And hear the questions
In her compassionate sighs.

Longing to hear her unconditional,
 "I love you,"
I'll have to wait until Grace
Gives me the final cue.

Different or Better

I cannot talk to you
Because I ask foolish questions,
But the Lord uses the foolish
Things to confound the wise.

I cannot converse with you,
I am wretched and sinful;
But let he who is without sin
Cast the first stone.

I cannot speak with you,
I have a different accent;
Do all birds have the same color
Or sing the same song?

I cannot talk with you
Because you're too judgmental;
Take the beam from your eyes
Before you give me a physical.

Does different mean worse,
Higher, or better?
Or does it give us
A chance to be wiser?

My Ride

*T*he baby is crying
        But the father does not hear;
It's dirty and needs
New shoes to wear.

The baby is hungry
But the mother makes no plea;
Its eyes are foggy,
It can hardly see.

The baby is choking
On a ton of greasy, grungy garbage,
But no one is hearing
Its loud but silent message.

"I take you to your lover,
To your work, and to your mother,
Although you give me neither
A nice vacuum nor a warm shower."

"I may embarrass you
When you least expect,
For cleanliness you swore
To resent and reject."

False Self-Image

I thought I was all that
Plus a floating ship,
I thought that with Christ
I had the optimum relationship.

I compared myself to my
Relatives and many a believer,
Thinking that I was
A worthy, willing worshipper.

Then one morning the sun shone
On the glass above my front door,
And on the windshield of my car,
Then I realized that I was a bore.

The light of the Son
And His piercing Word,
Forced me to crave
Cleansing from the Lord.

Now, my yardstick is the
Living Word of Almighty God;
The believers will never again
Be my scale and rod.

Exhortation

Stockpile

Remember your Creator
In the days of your youth,
Seek early, seek earnestly,
Seek the Way and the Truth.

What did young Joseph
Do in the seven years of plenty?
He planned and stockpiled
For the seven years of empty.

Do you stockpile wealth, time,
Prayer and love?
Store treasures in Christ;
Hide riches in things above.

Many seniors are like fish
Without water in retirement,
They have no earthly
Or heavenly investment.

Would you allow your children
To start from the floor?
When you look back,
Could you have saved more?

False Sun

I went to my bathroom
One morning and saw
A strong and bright sun
Shining through my window.

It was sending rays
Through branches and leaves,
Giving light to a spider
As it turned and weaved

Mr. Sun was traveling over a hill
As if just risen from slumber.
Honestly, I took the bait,
Hook, line, and floater.

Without warning the street light
Ceased to operate;
It could pretend no longer
For power it could not generate.

The real Sun came
To sit on His throne,
And gave victory, light,
And warmth to His own.

Beware! Many will say,
'I am the true Son and Friend,'
But time will reveal
Those who destroy or mend.

Missing Parents

I posed a question to my friend:
"Who has the most important job?"
"That's easy, a doctor saves lives."
I said, "Think again."

He smiled, "I am sure it's a pastor,
Because a pastor shows
The way to eternal life."
I answered, "Think again."

He paused for a moment,
Then declared "Oh, it's a farmer,
Because we cannot live without food."
I declared, "Try again."

He asked, "Could it be a soldier?
Life is worthless
Without freedom."
I responded, "Think no more."

Good parents not only
Help to produce life,
But lead the way to peace,
Despite chaos and strife.

They constantly teach,
Provide, and protect,
So that the love of the Savior
Their children may project.

The Butcher

What do you really do
By giving your daughter for a wife?
Have you thought about
The gun, the boat, or the knife?

You always think your marriage
Is going to be engulfed with euphoria,
But it often ends unexpectedly
With a serious case of pistoria.

You may be giving her away
Like a sheep to the slaughter,
To a decent and handsome
But barbarous, brutal butcher.

She could become a statistic in
The culture of female sacrifice;
The risk is like buying lottery,
Or gambling with cards and dice.

Sisters, discern as you look
For all the subtle threats;
Keep your eyes open
And "use sleep to mark death."

The enemy comes to kill, steal,
And destroy relationships,
To blight and murder children
By shrewdly launching battleships.

The Witch

W hat do you really do,
     By giving your son to be a husband?
Have you thought about the Gardener,
Anti-freeze and the magic wand?

You may be offering him,
Like a sheep to the slaughter,
To a lovely, and beautiful,
But wicked, weird witch.

This could possibly be an opportunity
For severe psychological torture,
Or a felony without any
Credible or definite closure.

Be careful to evaluate her
Chief goals and value system,
For without a true alliance
Your path will have a rough rhythm.

The enemy comes to disrupt,
Marginalize, and destroy
Each marriage, giving your children
A crooked, crude, and cruel heritage.

Evangelism

Don't Miss the Narrow Path Train

*I*f you miss the Narrow Path
Train from anywhere,
You will be trapped in a
Scorching cell for all eternity.

Traveling to a wedding reception
In Queens Village, New York,
I missed the 5:30 a.m. Path Train
At Newark Penn Station by a second.

In college, I lost a race
By a hundredth of a second;
Later in the year, I failed
A chemistry test by one percent.

After graduation, life was scary;
I missed my only job interview
Because my friend ate my message;
He said that it tasted like stew.

It got worse when my girlfriend
Walked away because of three words;
Frustration and disappointment
Pushed me to the bottle and the ward.

I was applying to Mr. Suicide,
But when I thought of my parents;
I caught the Narrow Path Train
By the simple Sinner's Prayer.

The Big One

The Big One is coming
Much sooner than you think;
Although it's a snail,
It'll be here before you blink.

Some say it'll hit California,
But China should watch the clock;
If she is not prepared,
She is an injured, drunk duck.

The 2004 Tsunami will look like a game
And Katrina a birthday party;
Hiroshima and Nagasaki cannot be
Likened to the Big One's agony.

They talk about biological
And chemical warfare,
But to the Big One,
None of these can compare.

Oprah, Diddy, or FEMA
Cannot give a helping hand,
Only Jesus' blood has provided
A foolproof evacuation plan.

Fifty Cent, or fifty three million bills,
Cannot take you past the pearly gates;
You may die trying, but only
On Jesus' work will the Father wait.

Europe and the Americas,
Antarctica and Asia,
Australia and Africa,
They will all hear from the Big One.

She struck in Noah's day,
But only eight found the Way;
Hitting Sodom and Gomorrah,
He captured the wife's tomorrow.

A third of the nations
Will be touched by a bomb,
Because their names were not
Found in the Book of the Lamb.

If you have not
The Prince of Peace,
You will be escorted
To a cold but fiery place.

Clothed but Naked

S tomach full but your soul
Is craving to be clothed;
Not with the linen you possess,
But with God's righteousness.

Regarding sword and shield,
You have been found lacking;
Without wealth and peace,
But gathering dollars and stacking.

Education, riches, fame, and skills
Cannot be substituted for His will;
His wisdom protects and prepares
You for all battles and spills.

Do you walk naked in the streets
To expose your weakness and shame?
So why travel on this lonely road
Without calling on Jesus' name?

Building houses and buying clothes
For the sick and needy,
But you're homeless and naked;
For His coming, you're not ready.

The Good Must Die

I was talking to a sincere
Retired veteran about
His need to accept Christ
Before his light went out.

He said that when he stands
Before God on the final day,
God will know that he was good
And helped many people on their way.

I said, "Good deeds cannot bring
Acceptance with a just God,
Neither will you be rejected
Because of your deeds that are bad."

I explained that salvation comes
Not through our works and goodness,
But it's a precious gift given through
Faith in Christ's love and righteousness.

Rest in Christ

I will not leave you comfortless,
You are safe in My arms;
Furthermore, I am in Him,
So there is no need for alarm.

Should a husband turn
His back on his wife?
It's like stabbing yourself
In the chest with a knife.

Your bills, dreams, problems,
Call out to Me;
I'll hold your hand,
With you, I will always be.

Can a mother divorce
Her precious daughter?
I am your husband!
I am your mother!

The Whistle Blower

Y ou must blow the Father's horn,
   Through this, children are born;
There are things you can do
To make your dreams come true.

Accept God's beloved Son,
That's the first step to battles won;
You cannot do this on your own,
Salvation comes through Christ alone.

Submit to Him while you're in
The great flood and wilderness;
Only a hardened arrow
Can spread the fire of His holiness.

Put your life in His hand
On the center of the steering wheel;
By yourself, you're powerless-
Without strength and zeal.

He'll press your finger
To make a thunderous sound
Because the train of death is on its way;
No traveler should go underground.

They who reject Him
To follow their own regulation
Will not escape, because only His
His pure blood secured salvation.

First Things First — or Lost

*D*on't put the cart
Before the horse;
Get the baton before
Starting the course.

Never reverse your car
Before looking behind.
Read all documents;
Don't sign as if you're blind.

Find self and assignment
Before choosing a mate;
Seek eternal things
Before it's too late.

First, seek to get your name
In the Lamb's Book of Life,
Before signing for a fine
Husband or a beautiful wife.

Second, keep searching
For the righteousness of God;
This is a recipe for favor
And all that is true and good.

Are You Ready?

Whether you are Michael,
Mary, Dianna, or Paul,
If you have not repented
You have accepted a fall

Toward the fiery tomb
Of an eternal cell,
Where the Prince of lies
Can ring your bell.

Rich, poor, Asian, Black,
Latino, Chinese, or White,
The Judge shall appear
Like a thief in the night.

When Noah built the ark,
They thought it was a joke;
Today, many are rejecting Christ
As they embrace crack and coke.

All have sinned
And missed His mark;
Shelter is in Christ,
He is now the open ark.

Are you waiting for
A friend or for sorrow?
Today is in your hand,
Don't bank on tomorrow.

Settle Your Account Now

C ash your check
And settle your account now,
You're serving others
But never to Jesus bow.

Many serve children
While others serve spouses;
Many serve careers,
While others serve houses.

Many serve the poor,
While others serve the sick,
But to serve the Almighty
We are not very quick.

Do not be like the serving,
Worrying, and fearful Martha
Who chose to do good
But ignore Him Who is better.

Time is flying to eternity,
Invalid will be your check,
For in a few months,
The bank may say, "I reject."

Cash your check now
And settle your account,
Give your heart to the Savior,
Then all your work will count.

I Saw Jesus on Stone Mountain

When I was in despair,
I saw Jesus on Stone Mountain;
He whispered, "Don't be afraid,
There is freedom at my fountain."

He gave me counsel for my mind
And shoes for my feet,
He said, "Son, don't ever
Be scared of the heat."

When I lost my job,
He explained, "Focus on
The covenant - I'll make you
Strong and resistant."

He did not scold me for
All that transpired,
He advised, "Only believe
And you'll be an arrow to be fired."

I saw Jesus in a shepherd
By the name of Simeon,
He declared, "God is your Father
So you're a royal son."

Where Are You Going?

I saw four of my classmates
In Kingston, Jamaica,
Just before they boarded
An airline to Atlanta.

Wayne said, "I am going
To New York for a family reunion,"
While Wendy bragged,
"I am going to marry my companion."

Richard declared, "I am going
To China on a mission for Christ,"
But Winsome said she was going
To collect a music award - her first.

They all boarded the plane
To catch connecting flights,
Twenty seconds into the air
Explosions destroyed all lights.

Where are they now?
Where are you going?

The Pencil

I chose a long pencil
To proclaim my Son's right,
Although it was sharpened,
It would not write.

I released that pencil
And used another;
It was short but willing,
It did not fume or falter.

Although received air,
Light, and nutrients,
The flower is still
Without consequence.

Do you want to be disregarded
Or used and be rewarded?
Singer, where is your song?
How long should I wait, how long?

Flower, where is your fruit?
Giver, where is your gift?
Quickly, gather the workers together-
So the burden is not too heavy to lift.

Warfare

My Dad is No King

The content of your genes
Determines your heredity,
So if your dad isn't a king,
How can you be royalty?

The blood of the fetus
Does not mix with the mother's
And all defining chromosomes
Are contributed by the father.

The prepared path produces
Your strongest inclination
And declares the essence
Of your purest imagination.

To decode meaning,
The question - Who are you?
Must be answered,
Then be conquered.

Cash your comprehensive check,
The ship has benefits attached;
The blessing and favor
Can never be matched.

Your name is authentic;
It cannot be erased.
The will is probated,
Urgently accept His grace.

Precious Bundle

What is the price,
Cost, and value
Of a pure, puny,
Precious bundle?

How much would you give
To get a bundle in your home?
Would you exchange a bundle
For a fancy vacation in Rome?

Are bundles sold
For bottles of wine?
Or are they given
In exchange for a dime?

My Friend paid for all
The bundles He could find
By putting His precious
Blood on the line.

Guilty but Innocent

*B*lood and water flowed
From His side,
So Compassion and Love
Could no longer hide.

Jealousy and hatred
Derailed a fair trial,
But He secured a line
That everyone can dial.

Found guilty, though
He was innocent,
He provides mercy
For those who repent.

Who Are You? 1

Y ou can either be wrong
Or you can be right;
A sheep without a shepherd
Or a child of the true Light.

Who are you and
What's your name?
Pity and inferiority
Should not be your game.

If you're royalty,
A child of the King,
You're his righteousness,
So you have a song to sing.

You're bought with a price,
You're not your own;
Or Jesus as Lord,
You have not known.

Would an ambassador walk
With guilt and a frown,
When in his home
A crown can be found?

You can either be wrong,
Or you can be right;
A sheep without a shepherd
Or a child of the true Light.

Scarred Body

*T*aking on a body
   For our cause,
He lived His life
With all the scars.

From everlasting, He chose
To live with this reality;
Will you look for
The marks in eternity?

Like a conch carrying
Its heavy shell,
He bore our sins
To save us from hell.

By purchasing redemption
With His broken body,
He presented us to
Our loving Daddy.

What Time Is It?

We should be aware of
  The time of day
Because we all need
To work and play.

Utilizing our talents
By carving our spaces,
We can traverse our paths
To complete our races.

Do we have enough
Gas In our tanks,
Or money to retire
Secure in banks?

We all need
To sink to our knees
Before eternity calls
And precious time flees.

Focus

S eriously, never gaze
While driving,
Nor lose sight of the
Ball while catching.

If focus is
Lost on a mask,
Your cross may be
Too huge a task.

Wander, blink, and
Worry for a second,
And the Deceiver may
Delay your mission.

Without focus, you cannot
Complete your race,
For detours and lapses
Will stifle your pace.

Gang Warfare

*E*ating the bait
Each hour of the day,
Hundreds and thousands
Miss the only Way.

They fall by starvation,
Cancer, and suicide,
By homicide and
Cruel infanticide.

The strategy is
To plunder humanity
Of honor, prosperity,
And a dignified eternity.

However, the cure is secured
By the Lamb Who was slain;
He created victory
Through obedience and pain.

Victory is in the broken
Body and the shed blood,
The words of your testimony,
The Spirit and the Word of God.

Who Are You? 2

*I*f you have found the Truth,
Walked in the Way, and received Life,
You are sealed by the Spirit
From a certain strife.

You are bought with a price,
You're without condemnation.

If you don't believe,
Read the prescription.

You are a perfect,
Precious pilgrim.

You're bold as a lion
And hard as diamond.

Blessed more than
A conqueror,
You're justified,
Sanctified,
To be glorified.

You're spirit with
A soul in a body,
A beautiful, bought
Bride.

Healed, helped, strengthened
By His righteous
Right hand.

A friend,
A child of the One True King.

Who are you?
As He is, so are you
In this world,
Joint heirs with Christ,
A golden pearl.

You are chosen,
The light of the world,
The salt of the earth,
You're of great worth.

You're the cherry of His eye,
You are breathing,
You're in Him,
You're loved.

Decision

You can sit on the bench,
or stand the fence,
But apathy and indecision
Cannot be your defense.

God or greed,
Life or death,
Blessing or curse,
Love or hate.

Faith or fear,
Mary or Martha,
Speak to or strike
The rock further.

You may walk naked,
Make your own crown,
Or allow the Lamb
To prepare your gown.

David or Goliath,
Law or grace,
It's a choice
You must face.

One God

*T*here are many gods
 In and around us,
But it's only the true God
We should trust.

Ishmael or Isaac,
Law or grace,
Struggling or resting
In a quiet place.

Where Do You Live?

H ouses are constructed
Everywhere,
In many a terrain
And atmosphere.

Some houses are built
On the Solid Rock
While others are built
On a huge, shifting block.

Some people live
In perilous and raging seas,
While others find a quiet
Stream on their knees.

Some people live in cells
With dark, dreadful deeds
Which they vowed
Not to repeat or sell.

Some live both
In the past and in fear;
They have no one on
Whom to cast their care.

Some people live under bridges,
Law, and condemnation,
But others live secure with
The seal of eternal salvation.

Some live in Love
And walk in the Light,
They live under grace
And give up the fight.

Some live with stress,
Anger, and sadness,
While others live with grace
And the gift of righteousness.

Some people live
In the secret place
Of the Most High.

Where do you live?

Case Dismissed

*I*t was a chilly day
    When I faced the judge
To present my case
In a huge, grey room.
I rehearsed my
Defense in my mind.

The kind judge explained
That the three pleas were:
Not guilty, no contest, or guilty.

It was interesting to note
That there was one offense
That the judge had no authority
To show leniency on, in his verdict.

My accuser took the stand
And opened a large grey book;
It was much larger than all the books
The other accusers used.

Several names were called
With many fines issued,
Threats made,
And advice given.

I knew my name would
Soon be called,
And my heart began to race
Like Usain Bolt.

The moment came;
My name echoed
Through the room,
So I walked to the front.
The judge asked, "Have you
Fixed the brakes?"
I said, "Yes."
And was about to present
My rehearsed defense
When the judge intervened,
"We believe you,
Your case is dismissed."

It was great joy
And relief for me
So I said "Thank you,"
To the judge and went
On my joyful way.

If you have fixed
The break, by faith
Through grace,
Your case is dismissed.

Tomorrow Will Never Come

Today and not tomorrow
Is the only time we are given
To secure our futures,

When we live in the future,
It's like sacrificing our goals
On the altar of the unknown.

When we worship tomorrow
It's like throwing life savers
After our dreams have perished.

When we live for tomorrow,
It's like making bids
After the auction is over.

When we rely on tomorrow,
It's like answering the Spirit's call
After time elapses and falls.

Tomorrow is not certain,
Tomorrow is not given,
Today is the present,
Today is a present.

The Blood

*I*f you are ill and doctors
  Can find no answer,
The blood of the Lamb
Is your joy and laughter.

If your depression baffles
The best-trained psychologist,
The blood of the Lamb
Is your power to be an optimist.

If your spirit is getting weak,
Asking, "Can I stand any longer?"
The blood of the Lamb
Is your solid Rock of Gibraltar.

If you face chaos and confusion
Saying, "My vision does not go far,"
The blood of the Lamb
Is your shining north star.

If life's trials are trying
To steal your family and sanity,
The blood of the Lamb
Is your anchor in calamity.

If life seems unbearable,
You may think, "What's the point?"
Be sure, you will be fine;
The blood of the Lamb is divine.

About the Author

Eric Kelly is a graduate of Walden University and the University of the West Indies. He is a former leader of the Evangelism Ministry of Heritage Fellowship Church in Reston, VA, where he is presently a youth leader. He lives in Herndon, VA, with his wife and two daughters.